Learn a Language!

See and Say
Spanish

by Claudia Oviedo

CAPSTONE PRESS
a capstone imprint

Published by Pebble, an imprint of Capstone
1710 Roe Crest Drive, North Mankato, Minnesota 56003
capstonepub.com

Library of Congress Cataloging-in-Publication Data is available on the Library of Congress website.

ISBN: 9780756581756 (hardcover)
ISBN: 9780756581947 (paperback)
ISBN: 9780756581794 (ebook PDF)

Summary: How do you ask someone how they're doing in Spanish? What's the Spanish word for *school*? With this book, curious kids will see and say simple words and phrases in Spanish.

Editorial Credits
Editor: Ericka Smith; Designer: Sarah Bennett; Media Researcher: Svetlana Zhurkin; Production Specialist: Katy LaVigne

Image Credits
Dreamstime: Rodrigo Vargas, 14 (top); Getty Images: aldomurillo, 22 (bottom left), Alejandra Paola De la Cruz Lopez, 25 (bottom right), Antonio_Diaz, 7 (bottom left), Ariel Skelley, 26 (bottom), FabrikaCr, 5 (middle right), 11 (top right), FG Trade Latin, 19 (bottom left), GM Visuals, 16 (bottom), Guadalupe Rojas, 5 (middle left), 25 (top right), Hector Vivas, 23 (bottom), ImagineGolf, 15 (bottom right), Jose Luis Pelaez Inc, 7 (top), 17 (middle), Jules Ingall, 27 (top), M Swiet Productions, 25 (bottom left), mofles, 17 (bottom left), ranplett, 16 (top), stellalevi, 4, Vladimir Mironov, 10 (bottom); Shutterstock: Africa Studio, 17 (bottom right), Anton_Ivanov, 18 (middle right), Arkadij Schell, 21 (middle right), asharkyu, cover (middle left), asife, 31 (middle), bergamont, 29 (middle right), Boonchuay Promjiam, 29 (bottom left), Bruno_Doinel, 19 (middle), Carolina Arroyo, 10 (middle), Chayanit Itthipongmaetee, 19 (top right), clicksdemexico, 5 (top), 15 (bottom left and middle), 22 (top right), Digital Media Pro, 23 (top left), DnD-Production, 13 (bottom), ehudson, 20 (bottom), Elizabeth_0102, 29 (middle left), Enrique20k, 19 (bottom right), Eric Isselee, 12 (top left and bottom right), 13 (top right), Eternar, 26 (middle right), FamVeld, 30 (middle left), Fascinadora, 30 (middle), Fernanda_Reyes, 8, Fotofermer, 28 (bottom left), Guajillo studio, 11 (middle), halimqd (speech bubble and burst), cover and throughout, Ildi Papp, 10 (top), Inspired By Maps, 15 (top), Irina Wilhauk, 31 (top), Ivanova N, 12 (top right), Krakenimages, 7 (bottom right), Lorenza Ochoa, 18 (middle left), Magnia (lined texture), cover and throughout, Marcos Castillo, 14 (bottom), 22 (bottom right), Mateusz Atroszko, 21 (top), Matt Jeppson, 13 (middle right), Matthias G. Ziegler, cover (bottom right), 1, Monkey Business Images, 9, Muenchbach, 17 (top), Naypong Studio, 29 (top), Nekomura, 19 (top left), nukeaf, 24, Octavio Hoyos, 18 (bottom), oksana.perkins, 20 (middle), oksana2010, 28 (top right), PageSeven, 11 (top left), photomaster, 13 (top left), Pierrette Guertin, 26 (middle left), Prill, 27 (bottom), Purple Clouds, cover (bottom left), Ricardo JG, 25 (top left), Roman Samborskyi, 7 (middle), Ruslan Huzau, 22 (top left), Ruth Black, 30 (top, middle right, and bottom), 31 (middle right, middle left, and bottom), Salmonnegro-Stock, 21 (middle left), Santiago Castillo Chomel, 20 (top), spiharu.u (spot line art), cover and throughout, Stephen Coburn, 6, Suriel Ramzal, 18 (top), Tim UR, 28 (top left), Tsekhmister, 12 (bottom left), 13 (middle left), Vangert, 28 (bottom right), Victor M. Velazquez, cover (top right), wavebreakmedia, 23 (top right), winphong, 29 (bottom right), Yuricazac, cover (top left)

Printed and bound in China. PO5834

Table of Contents

The Spanish Language

The Spanish people speak today started in northern Spain about 1,500 years ago. Now, Spanish is an official language in 21 countries! For about 360 million people, Spanish is the first language they learned to speak.

An official language is a language that many people in a country speak. It might be used by the government, at schools, and in other important places.

How to Use This Book

Some words and phrases complete a sentence.
Those will appear in bold.

`English` **I like . . .**
`Spanish` Me gusta . . .
`Say It!` meh goo-stah

+

`English` **dancing.**
`Spanish` bailar.
`Say It!` bai-lahr

Others give you the name for a person,
place, thing, or idea.

`English` spring
`Spanish` primavera
`Say It!` pree-mah-veh-rah

`English` milk
`Spanish` leche
`Say It!` leh-cheh

Meet Chatty Cat! Chatty Cat will show you how
to say the words and phrases in this book.

Greetings and Phrases

Spanish Saludos y Frases

Say It!  sah-loo-dohs ee frah-sehs

English Hello!

Spanish ¡Hola!

Say It! oh-lah

English My name is . . .

Spanish Mi nombre es . . .

Say It! mee nom-breh es

English What's your name?

Spanish ¿Cuál es tu nombre?

Say It! kwahl es too nom-breh

English How are you?

Spanish ¿Cómo estás?

Say It! koh-moh es-tahs

English I am fine.

Spanish Estoy bien.

Say It! es-toy bee-en

English Nice to meet you.

Spanish Gusto en conocerte.

Say It! 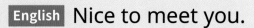 goos-toh en koh-noh-ser-teh

English Please.
Spanish Por favor.
Say It! 🐱 por fah-vor

English Thank you!
Spanish ¡Gracias!
Say It! 🐱 grah-syas

English You're welcome!
Spanish ¡De nada!
Say It! 🐱 deh nah-dah

English Goodbye!
Spanish ¡Adiós!
Say It! 🐱 ah-dyohs

English See you later!
Spanish ¡Hasta luego!
Say It! 🐱 ahs-tah lway-go

English Yes.
Spanish Sí.
Say It! 🐱 see

English No.
Spanish No.
Say It! 🐱 noh

Family

English **Here is . . .**
Spanish Aquí está . . .
Say It! ah-kee es-tah

English **my mother.**
Spanish mi madre.
Say It! mee mah-dreh

English **my father.**
Spanish mi padre.
Say It! mee pah-dreh

English **my sister.**
Spanish mi hermana.
Say It! mee ehr-mah-nah

English **my brother.**
Spanish mi hermano
Say It! mee ehr-mah-noh

English **my aunt.**
Spanish mi tía.
Say It! mee tee-ah

English **my uncle.**
Spanish mi tío.
Say It! mee tee-oh

English **my cousin.**
Spanish mi primo. (boy)
Say It! mee pree-moh
Spanish mi prima. (girl)
Say It! mee pree-mah

English **my grandmother.**
Spanish mi abuela.
Say It! mee ah-bweh-lah

English **my grandfather.**
Spanish mi abuelo.
Say It! mee ah-bweh-loh

Food

Spanish Comida
Say It! koh-mee-dah

English **I'm hungry. I want . . .**
Spanish Tengo hambre. Quiero . . .
Say It! 🐱 tehn-goh ahm-breh kee-eh-roh

English **breakfast.**
Spanish desayuno.
Say It! 🐱 deh-sah-yoo-noh

English eggs
Spanish huevos
Say It! 🐱 oo-eh-vohs

English sausage
Spanish chorizo
Say It! 🐱 cho-ree-zoh

English **lunch.**
Spanish comida.
Say It! 🐱 koh-mee-dah

English sandwich
Spanish torta
Say It! 🐱 tor-tah

English **dinner.**
Spanish cena.
Say It! 🐱 seh-nah

English fried pork
Spanish carnitas
Say It! 🐱 car-nee-tahs

English **a snack.**

Spanish una botana.

Say It! oo-nah bow-ta-nah

English pineapple

Spanish piña

Say It! pee-nyah

English milk

Spanish leche

Say It! leh-cheh

English bread

Spanish pan

Say It! pahn

English Mexican turnip

Spanish jícama

Say It! hee-kah-mah

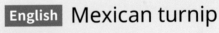

Many Mexican foods have become so popular that they are known around the world by their Spanish names—no translation necessary. These include *tacos*, *tamales*, and *enchiladas*.

Animals

Spanish Animales

Say It! 🐱 ah-nee-mah-les

English a cat

Spanish un gato

Say It! 🐱 oon gah-toh

English a dog

Spanish un perro

Say It! 🐱 oon peh-roh

English a horse

Spanish un caballo

Say It! 🐱 oon kah-bah-yoh

English a chicken

Spanish una gallina

Say It! 🐱 oo-nah gah-yee-nah

English a fish

Spanish un pez

Say It! 🐱 oon pehs

English a bird

Spanish un pájaro

Say It! 🐱 oon pah-hah-roh

English a pig

Spanish un cerdo

Say It! 🐱 oon sehr-doh

English a frog

Spanish una rana

Say It! 🐱 oo-nah rah-nah

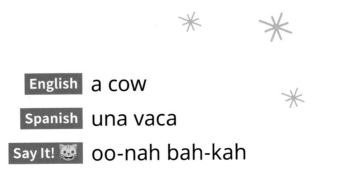

English a cow

Spanish una vaca

Say It! 🐱 oo-nah bah-kah

13

At Home

Spanish **En Casa**
Say It! 🐱 ehn kah-sah

English **a kitchen**
Spanish **una cocina**
Say It! 🐱 oo-nah koh-see-nah

English **a window**
Spanish **una ventana**
Say It! 🐱 oo-nah behn-tah-nah

English **a table**
Spanish **una mesa**
Say It! 🐱 oo-nah meh-sah

English **a chair**
Spanish **una silla**
Say It! 🐱 oo-nah see-yah

English **a living room**
Spanish **una sala**
Say It! 🐱 oo-nah sah-lah

English **a couch**
Spanish **un sofá**
Say It! 🐱 oon soh-fah

English **a cell phone**
Spanish **un teléfono celular**
Say It! 🐱 oon teh-leh-foh-noh sel-oo-lahr

English **a computer**
Spanish **una computadora**
Say It! 🐱 oo-nah kohm-poo-tah-doh-rah

English a bedroom

Spanish una recámara

Say It! 🐱 oo-nah reh-kah-mah-rah

English a bed

Spanish una cama

Say It! 🐱 oo-nah kah-mah

English a door

Spanish una puerta

Say It! 🐱 oo-nah pwehr-tah

English a bathroom

Spanish un baño

Say It! 🐱 oon bah-nyoh

English a sink

Spanish un lavabo

Say It! 🐱 oon lah-vah-boh

English a toilet

Spanish un inodoro

Say It! 🐱 oon ee-noh-doh-roh

English a bathtub

Spanish una bañera

Say It! 🐱 oo-nah bah-nyeh-rah

15

Clothing

Spanish Ropa
Say It! roh-pah

English I am wearing . . .
Spanish Llevo puesto . . . (boy)
Say It! yeh-voh pwehs-toh
Spanish Llevo puesta . . . (girl)
Say It! yeh-voh pwehs-tah

English **a shirt.**
Spanish una camisa.
Say It! oo-nah kah-mee-sah

English **pants.**
Spanish pantalones.
Say It! pahn-tah-loh-nes

English **a hat.**
Spanish un gorro.
Say It! oon goh-roh

English **a coat.**
Spanish un abrigo.
Say It! oon ah-bree-goh

English **a sweatshirt.**

Spanish una sudadera.

Say It! 🐱 oo-nah soo-dah-deh-rah

English **a dress.**

Spanish un vestido.

Say It! 🐱 oon vehs-tee-doh

English **shoes.**

Spanish zapatos.

Say It! 🐱 sah-pah-tohs

English **a skirt.**

Spanish una falda.

Say It! 🐱 oo-nah fahl-dah

English **socks.**

Spanish calcetines.

Say It! 🐱 kahl-seh-tee-nes

17

In the Neighborhood

Spanish En la Vecindad

Say It! 🐱 ehn lah veh-seen-dahd

English an apartment building

Spanish un edificio de apartamentos

Say It! 🐱 oon eh-dee-fee-see-oh deh ah-pahr-tah-mehn-tohs

English a street

Spanish una calle

Say It! 🐱 oo-nah kah-yeh

English a grocery store

Spanish un mercado

Say It! 🐱 oon mehr-kah-doh

English a house

Spanish una casa

Say It! 🐱 oo-nah kah-sah

English a hospital

Spanish un hospital

Say It! 🐱 oon oh-spee-tahl

English a post office

Spanish una oficina de correos

Say It! 🐱 oo-nah oh-fee-see-nah deh koh-reh-oh

English a library

Spanish una biblioteca

Say It! 🐱 oo-nah bee-blee-oh-teh-kah

English a bus stop

Spanish una parada de camión

Say It! 🐱 oo-nah pah-rah-dah deh kah-mee-ohn

English a school

Spanish una escuela

Say It! 🐱 oo-nah ehs-kweh-lah

English a park

Spanish un parque

Say It! 🐱 oon pahr-keh

Transportation

Spanish Transporte

Say It! 🐱 trahns-por-teh

English a car

Spanish un carro

Say It! 🐱 oon kah-roh

English a bus

Spanish un camión

Say It! 🐱 oon kah-mee-ohn

English a boat

Spanish un barco

Say It! 🐱 oon bahr-koh

English a train

Spanish un tren

Say It! 🐱 oon trehn

English an airplane

Spanish un avión

Say It! 🐱 oon ah-vee-ohn

English a bicycle

Spanish una bicicleta

Say It! 🐱 oo-nah
bee-see-kleh-tah

English a truck

Spanish una camioneta

Say It! 🐱 oo-nah kah-mee-
ohn-eh-tah

In Mexico, the word *camioneta* refers to several types of vehicles. These include pickup trucks, vans, SUVs, and station wagons.

Hobbies

Spanish Pasatiempos
Say It! 🐱 pah-sah-tee-em-pohs

English I like . . .
Spanish Me gusta . . .
Say It! 🐱 meh goo-stah

English **singing.**
Spanish cantar.
Say It! 🐱 kahn-tahr

English **dancing.**
Spanish bailar.
Say It! 🐱 bai-lahr

English **painting.**
Spanish pintar.
Say It! 🐱 peen-tahr

English **swimming.**
Spanish nadar.
Say It! 🐱 nah-dahr

English **soccer.**

Spanish fútbol.

Say It! 🐱 foot-bohl

English a ball

Spanish una pelota

Say It! 🐱 oo-nah peh-loh-tah

English **reading.**

Spanish leer.

Say It! 🐱 leh-ehr

English a book

Spanish un libro

Say It! 🐱 oon lee-broh

English **wrestling.**

Spanish lucha.

Say It! 🐱 loo-chah

Wrestling, known as *lucha libre*, is big in Mexico. As a hobby, most people prefer watching it to getting in the ring.

Days of the Week

Spanish Días de la Semana

Say It! dee-ahs deh lah seh-mah-nah

English **Today is . . .**

Spanish Hoy es . . .

Say It! oy ehs

English **Monday.**

Spanish Lunes.

Say It! loo-nes

English **Tuesday.**

Spanish Martes.

Say It! mahr-tes

English **Wednesday.**

Spanish Miércoles.

Say It! mee-ehr-koh-les

English **Thursday.**

Spanish Jueves.

Say It! hweh-ves

English **Friday.**

Spanish Viernes.

Say It! vee-ehr-nes

English **Saturday.**

Spanish Sábado.

Say It! sah-bah-doh

English **Sunday.**

Spanish Domingo.

Say It! doh-meen-goh

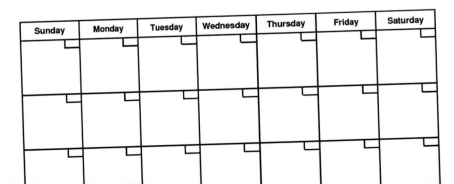

Sunday	Monday	Tuesday	Wednesday	Thursday	Friday	Saturday

Seasons

English winter

Spanish invierno

Say It! 🐱 een-vyehr-noh

English spring

Spanish primavera

Say It! 🐱 pree-mah-veh-rah

English summer

Spanish verano

Say It! 🐱 veh-rah-noh

English fall

Spanish otoño

Say It! 🐱 oh-toh-nyoh

Weather

Spanish Tiempo
Say It!  tee-em-poh

English **It is . . .**
Spanish Está . . .
Say It! es-tah

English **raining.**
Spanish lloviendo.
Say It! yoh-vee-ehn-doh

English **windy.**
Spanish ventoso.
Say It! vehn-toh-soh

English **cold.**
Spanish frío.
Say It! free-oh

English **snowing.**
Spanish nevando.
Say It! neh-vahn-doh

English **hot.**
Spanish caliente.
Say It! 🐱 kah-lee-en-teh

English **sunny.**
Spanish soleado.
Say It! 🐱 soh-leh-ah-doh

English **cloudy.**
Spanish nublado.
Say It! 🐱 noo-blah-doh

Colors

Spanish Colores

Say It! 🐱 koh-lohr-es

English red

Spanish rojo

Say It! 🐱 roh-hoh

English pink

Spanish rosita

Say It! 🐱 roh-see-tah

English green

Spanish verde

Say It! 🐱 vehr-deh

English orange

Spanish anaranjado

Say It! 🐱 a-nah-rahn-hah-doh

English blue
Spanish azul
Say It! 🐱 ah-sool

English yellow
Spanish amarillo
Say It! 🐱 ah-mah-ree-yoh

English purple
Spanish morado
Say It! 🐱 moh-rah-doh

English black
Spanish negro
Say It! 🐱 neh-groh

English white
Spanish blanco
Say It! 🐱 blahn-koh

29

Numbers

Spanish Números

Say It! 🐱 noo-mer-ohs

1

English one

Spanish uno

Say It! 🐱 oo-noh

2

English two

Spanish dos

Say It! 🐱 dohs

3

English three

Spanish tres

Say It! 🐱 trehs

4

English four

Spanish cuatro

Say It! 🐱 kwah-troh

5

English five

Spanish cinco

Say It! 🐱 seen-ko

6

English six

Spanish seis

Say It! 🐱 sehs

7

English seven

Spanish siete

Say It! 🐱 syeh-teh

8

English eight

Spanish ocho

Say It! 🐱 oh-choh

9

English nine

Spanish nueve

Say It! 🐱 nweh-veh

10

English ten

Spanish diez

Say It! 🐱 dyehs

About the Translator

Claudia Oviedo writes for children under various names. She grew up on the U.S.-Mexico border. Spanish was her first language.